National Military Strategy
of the United States of America
2004

A Strategy for Today; A Vision for Tomorrow

Table of Contents

Foreword

The "National Military Strategy" conveys my message to the Joint Force on the strategic direction the Armed Forces of the United States should follow to support the National Security and Defense Strategies in this time of war. This document describes the ways and means to **protect** the United States, **prevent** conflict and surprise attack and **prevail** against adversaries who threaten our homeland, deployed forces, allies and friends. Success rests on three priorities:

First, while protecting the United States we must **win the War on Terrorism**. The attacks of 11 September 2001 demonstrated that our liberties are vulnerable. The prospect of future attacks, potentially employing weapons of mass destruction, makes it imperative we act now to stop terrorists before they can attack again. We must continue to root out transnational terrorist networks, sever their connections with state sponsors, eliminate their bases of operation, counter dangerous proliferation and establish a global antiterrorism environment. This mission requires the full integration of all instruments of national power, the cooperation and participation of friends and allies and the support of the American people.

Second, we will **enhance our ability to fight as a joint force**. Joint teamwork is an integral part of our culture and focus as we develop leaders, organizations, systems and doctrine. We must continue to strengthen trust and confidence among the Service components that comprise the Joint Force. Enhancing joint warfighting requires the integration of our Active and Reserve Components and our civilian work force to create a seamless total force that can meet future challenges. We must strengthen collaboration among our joint forces, agencies at all levels of government and multinational partners. Key to such collaboration is an improved ability to collect, process and share information.

Third, we will **transform the Armed Forces** "in stride" – fielding new capabilities and adopting new operational concepts while actively taking the fight to terrorists. Transformation requires a combination of technology, intellect and cultural adjustments – adjustments that reward innovation and creativity. In-stride transformation will ensure US forces emerge from the struggle against terrorism with our joint force fully prepared to meet future global challenges.

The NMS serves to focus the Armed Forces on maintaining US leadership in a global community that is challenged on many fronts – from countering the threat of global terrorism to fostering emerging democracies. In this environment, US presence and commitment to partners are essential. Our Armed Forces, operating at home and abroad, in peace and war, will continue to serve as a constant, visible reminder of US resolve to protect common interests. Our dedication to security and stability ensures that the United States is viewed as an indispensable partner, encouraging other nations to join us in helping make the world not just safer, but better.

RICHARD B. MYERS
Chairman
of the Joint Chiefs of Staff

Executive Summary

Chairman's Intent
Our challenge for the coming year and beyond is to stay the course in the War on Terrorism as we continue to transform our Armed Forces to conduct future joint operations. We cannot afford to let our recent successes cause us to lose focus or lull us into satisfaction with our current capabilities. The war is not over, and there is still dangerous work to do. To meet this challenge, we continue to focus on three priorities: winning the War on Terrorism, enhancing joint warfighting and transforming for the future.

Strategic Guidance
The National Military Strategy is guided by the goals and objectives contained in the President's "National Security Strategy" and serves to implement the Secretary of Defense's 2004 "National Defense Strategy of the United States of America."

The Role of the NMS
The NMS provides focus for military activities by defining a set of interrelated military objectives from which the Service Chiefs and combatant commanders identify desired capabilities and against which CJCS assesses risk.

Key Aspects of the Security Environment
- A Wider Range of Adversaries
- A More Complex and Distributed Battlespace
- Technology Diffusion and Access

Principles guiding the development of the Joint Force
- Agility
- Decisiveness
- Integration

Military Objectives
The NMS establishes three military objectives that support the National Defense Strategy:

- Protect the United States Against External Attacks and Aggression
- Prevent Conflict and Surprise Attack
- Prevail Against Adversaries.

Desired Attributes of the Force
- Fully Integrated
- Expeditionary
- Networked
- Decentralized
- Adaptable
- Decision Superiority
- Lethality

Capabilities and Functions
- Applying Force
- Deploying and Sustaining Military Capabilities
- Securing Battlespace
- Achieving Decision Superiority

Designing and Sizing the Force
Executing the NMS requires a force able to generate decisive effects in any contingency and sustain multiple, overlapping operations. The force must have the capabilities necessary to create and preserve an enduring peace.

Joint Vision for Future Warfighting
Sustaining and increasing the qualitative military advantages the United States enjoys today will require transformation - a transformation achieved by combining technology, intellect and cultural changes across the joint community. The goal is Full Spectrum Dominance – the ability to control any situation or defeat any adversary across the range of military operations.

I. Introduction

The National Military Strategy (NMS) supports the aims of the National Security Strategy (NSS) and implements the 2004 National Defense Strategy (NDS). It describes the Armed Forces' plan to achieve military objectives in the near term and provides the vision for ensuring they remain decisive in the future.

A. Strategic Guidance

1. The National Security Strategy

The President's NSS affirms the Nation's commitment to "help make the world not just safer but better." This requires victory in the War on Terrorism (WOT) – a victory that is enduring and contributes to defending, preserving and extending the peace. The NSS directs an active strategy to counter transnational terrorist networks, rogue nations and aggressive states that possess or are working to gain weapons of mass destruction or effect (WMD/E). [1] It emphasizes activities to foster relationships among US allies, partners and friends. Such relationships support efforts to strike globally at terrorist organizations and create conditions inhospitable to terrorism and rogue regimes. The NSS highlights the need to retain and improve capabilities to prevent attacks against the United States, work cooperatively with other nations and multinational organizations and transform America's national security institutions.

2. The 2004 National Defense Strategy

The 2004 NDS supports the NSS by establishing a set of overarching defense objectives that guide the Department's security activities and provide direction for the National Military Strategy. The NDS objectives serve as links between military activities and those of other government agencies in pursuit of national goals. The Department must take action to secure the United States from direct attack and counter, at a safe distance, those who seek to harm the country. The Department must work to secure strategic access to key regions, lines of communication and the "global commons" of international waters, airspace, space and cyberspace. Defense activities must help establish

> Four Defense objectives will guide DOD security activities:
>
> - Secure the United States from direct attack.
> - Secure strategic access and retain global freedom of action.
> - Establish security conditions conducive to a favorable international order.
> - Strengthen alliances and partnerships to contend with common challenges.
>
> *2004 National Defense Strategy*

security conditions favorable to the United States and its partners while working to expand the community of like-minded nations. The Department will also work to strengthen alliances and partnerships by helping other nations increase their ability to defend themselves and protect common security interests.

---

[1] The term WMD/E relates to a broad range of adversary capabilities that pose potentially devastating impacts. WMD/E includes chemical, biological, radiological, nuclear, and enhanced high explosive weapons as well as other, more asymmetrical "weapons". They may rely more on disruptive impact than destructive kinetic effects. For example, cyber attacks on US commercial information systems or attacks against transportation networks may have a greater economic or psychological effect than a relatively small release of a lethal agent.

The NDS focuses Department activities on actions that assure allies and friends, dissuade potential adversaries, deter aggression and counter coercion and defeat adversaries. These interconnected activities promote close cooperation with those committed to the principles of freedom, democracy and opportunity. The 2004 NDS provides four guidelines for implementing the strategy – create an active defense-in-depth; conduct continuous transformation; adopt a capabilities-based approach; and manage risks. These guidelines will structure strategic planning and decision-making across all segments of the Department.

B. The Role of the National Military Strategy

The NMS derives objectives, missions and capability requirements from an analysis of the NSS, the NDS and the security environment. The NSS and NDS provide a broad strategic context for employing military capabilities in concert with other instruments of national power. The NMS provides focus for military activities by defining a set of interrelated military objectives and joint operating concepts from which the Service Chiefs and combatant commanders identify desired capabilities and against which the Chairman of the Joint Chiefs of Staff assesses risk.

The NSS establishes homeland security as the first priority of the Nation. The Armed Forces' role in homeland security is complex, combining actions overseas and at home to **protect the United States**. Our first line of defense is abroad and includes mutually supporting activities with US allies to counter threats close to their source. Closer to home, the Armed Forces use their capabilities to secure strategic air, land, sea and space approaches to the United States and its territory. When directed, the Armed Forces employ military capabilities at home to protect the nation, the domestic population and critical infrastructure from direct attack. Protecting the United States also requires integrating military capabilities with other government and law enforcement agencies to manage the consequences of an attack or natural disaster.

The President and Secretary of Defense continue to highlight the increasingly dangerous nature and capabilities of adversaries. The threat posed by adversaries, especially those that possess WMD/E, is so great that the United States must adopt a global posture and take action to **prevent conflict and surprise attack**. Achieving this objective includes actions to shape the security environment in ways that enhance and expand multinational partnerships. Strong alliances and coalitions contribute to mutual security, tend to deter aggression, and help set conditions for success in combat if deterrence fails. Preventing conflict and surprise attack is not, however, solely defensive. The potentially catastrophic impact of an attack against the United States, its allies and its interests may necessitate actions in self-defense to preempt adversaries before they can attack.

Both the NSS and 2004 NDS envision a future environment that is safer and better than today. When called upon, the military must be prepared to contribute to this goal through campaigns to **prevail against adversaries**. While the Armed Forces' foremost task is to fight and win wars, the character of conflict has changed, necessitating capabilities to defeat a wide range of adversaries – from states to non-

2

state actors. The Armed Force must have the capability to swiftly defeat adversaries in overlapping campaigns while preserving the option to expand operations in one of those campaigns to achieve more comprehensive objectives. Prevailing against adversaries includes integrating all instruments of national power within a campaign to set the conditions for an enduring victory.

Achieving the objectives of **protect**, **prevent** and **prevail** requires connected joint operating concepts (JOCs) that provide direction on how the joint force will operate and a foundation for defining military capabilities. The JOCs describe how the Joint Force conducts key missions and are supported by functional concepts of **force application**, **protection**, **focused logistics**, **battlespace awareness** and **command and control**. The JOCs serve to guide the continuous transformation of the Armed Forces and provide a key linkage to the Armed Forces' vision[2] for future joint warfighting. This vision establishes the ultimate goal of the transformed force – the ability to achieve full spectrum dominance across the range of military operations.

Campaigns

- Campaigns to "swiftly defeat" the efforts of adversaries are undertaken to achieve a circumscribed set of objectives aimed at altering an adversary's unacceptable behavior or policies, swiftly denying an adversary's operational or strategic objectives, preventing attacks or uncontrolled conflict escalation and/or rapidly reestablishing security conditions favorable to the United States and its partners.

- Campaigns to "win decisively" are undertaken to bring about fundamental, favorable change in a crisis region and create enduring results. They likely entail lengthy periods of both major combat and stability operations; require regime change, defense, or restoration; and will include significant investments of the nation's resources and time.

2004 National Defense Strategy

Achieving the objectives of the NMS in an uncertain and complex environment requires a capabilities-based approach to force design and planning that focuses less on a specific adversary or where a conflict might occur and more on how an adversary might fight. This capabilities-based approach uses operating concepts to drive planning and to guide the development of warfighting capabilities. It ensures the joint force can adapt and succeed across a broad range of scenarios. This approach must anticipate and rapidly adjust to changes in the security environment to ensure the United States improves its qualitative advantage over a more diverse set of adversaries – now and in the future.

The objectives of the NMS help define attributes and capabilities that the Joint Force requires and directly contribute to objectives of the 2004 NDS. These attributes and capabilities are important in determining the required size and design of the Armed Forces. Protecting the United States, preventing conflict and surprise attacks, and prevailing against adversaries will require forces appropriately sized and shaped in accordance with the NDS force-planning construct. The force must be sized to defend the US homeland while continuing to operate in and from four forward regions to deter aggression and coercion and set conditions for future operations. Even when committed to a limited number of lesser contingencies, the Armed Forces must retain the capability to swiftly defeat adversaries in two overlapping military campaigns.

---

[2] The NMS integrates the document formerly known as "Joint Vision."

Additionally, when the President calls for an enduring result in one of the two, the force must have the capability and capacity to win decisively.

Combatant commands must consider the effect of their current posture when undertaking new operations. They will operate within a baseline security posture that includes the WOT and other ongoing operations from which they may be unable or unwilling to disengage. Planners must, therefore account for WOT campaign objectives when developing their force requirements.

C. Key Aspects of the Security Environment

The United States faces a number of dangerous and pervasive threats. Traditional, irregular, catastrophic, and disruptive challenges will require the Armed Forces to adjust quickly and decisively to change and anticipate emerging threats. Three key aspects of the security environment have unique implications for executing this military strategy and will drive the development of concepts and capabilities that ensure success in future operations.

1. A Wider Range of Adversaries

Adversaries capable of threatening the United States, its allies, and its interests range from states to non-state organizations to individuals. There are states with traditional

> ### Persistent and Emerging Challenges
>
> **Traditional** challenges are largely represented by states employing legacy and advanced military capabilities and recognizable military forces, in long-established, well-known forms of military competition and conflict.
>
> **Irregular** challenges are unconventional methods adopted and employed by non-state and state actors to counter stronger state opponents.
>
> **Catastrophic** challenges involve the surreptitious acquisition, possession, and possible terrorist or rogue employment of WMD or methods producing WMD-like effects.
>
> **Disruptive** future challenges are those likely to emanate from competitors developing, possessing, and employing breakthrough technological capabilities intended to supplant an opponent's advantages in particular operational domains.
>
> *2004 National Defense Strategy*

military forces and advanced systems, including cruise and ballistic missiles, which could seek to control key regions of the world. A few of these states are 'rogues' that violate treaties, secretly pursue and proliferate WMD/E, reject peaceful resolution of disputes and display callous disregard for their citizens. Some of these states sponsor terrorists, providing them financial support, sanctuary and access to dangerous capabilities. There are non-state actors, including terrorist networks, international criminal organizations and illegal armed groups that menace stability and security. Even some individuals may have the means and will to disrupt international order. Some of these adversaries are politically unconstrained and, particularly in the case of non-state actors, may be less susceptible to traditional means of deterrence. Adversaries increasingly seek asymmetric capabilities and will use them in innovative ways. They will avoid US strengths like precision strike and seek to counter US power projection capabilities by creating anti-access environments. Such adversaries will target civilian populations, economic centers and symbolic locations as a way to attack US political will and resolve.

This volatile mix of challenges requires new methods of deterrence and operational approaches to defeat these threats should deterrence fail. Intelligence systems must allow commanders to understand enemy intent, predict threat actions, and detect adversary movements, providing them the time necessary to take preventive measures. Long before conflict occurs these intelligence systems must help provide a more thorough understanding of adversaries' motivations, goals and organizations to determine effective deterrent courses of action. There may, however, be adversaries who remain undeterred. Should they acquire WMD/E or dangerous asymmetric capabilities, or demonstrate the intent to mount a surprise attack, the United States must be prepared to prevent them from striking.

2. A More Complex and Distributed Battlespace

Adversaries threaten the United States throughout a complex battlespace, extending from critical regions overseas to the homeland and spanning the global commons of international airspace, waters, space and cyberspace. There exists an "arc of instability" stretching from the Western Hemisphere, through Africa and the Middle East and extending to Asia. There are areas in this arc that serve as breeding grounds for threats to our interests. Within these areas rogue states provide sanctuary to terrorists, protecting them from surveillance and attack. Other adversaries take advantage of ungoverned space and under-governed territories from which they prepare plans, train forces and launch attacks. These ungoverned areas often coincide with locations of illicit activities; such coincidence creates opportunities for hostile coalitions of criminal elements and ideological extremists. The United States will conduct operations in widely diverse locations – from densely populated urban areas located in littoral regions to remote, inhospitable and austere locations. Military operations in this complex environment may be dramatically different than the high intensity combat missions for which US forces routinely train. While US Armed Forces' will continue to emphasize precision, speed, lethality and distributed operations, commanders must expect and plan for the possibility that their operations will produce unintended 2nd- and 3rd-order effects. For example, US forces can precisely locate, track, and destroy discrete targets to reduce collateral damage and conclude operations as quickly as possible. Operations that rely on precision may result in large elements of an adversary's military remaining intact and segments of the population unaffected. Commanders must prepare to operate in regions where pockets of resistance remain and there exists the potential for continued combat operations amidst a large number of non-combatants.

This battlespace places unique demands on military organizations and interagency partners, requiring more detailed coordination and synchronization of activities both overseas and at home. Our experiences in Afghanistan and Iraq highlight the need for a comprehensive strategy to achieve longer-term national goals and objectives. The United States must adopt an "active defense-in-depth" that merges joint force, interagency, international non-governmental organizations, and multinational capabilities in a synergistic manner. This defense does not rely solely on passive measures. The United States must enhance security at home while actively patrolling strategic approaches and extending defensive capabilities well beyond US borders. An effective defense-in-depth must also include the capability to strike swiftly at any target around the globe using forces at home as well as forward-based, forward-deployed and rotational forces.

3. *Technology Diffusion and Access*

Global proliferation of a wide range of technology and weaponry will affect the character of future conflict. Dual-use civilian technologies, especially information technologies, high-resolution imagery and global positioning systems are widely available. These relatively low cost, commercially available technologies will improve the disruptive and destructive capabilities of a wide range of state and non-state actors. Advances in automation and information processing will allow some adversaries to locate and attack targets both overseas and in the United States. Software tools for network-attack, intrusion and disruption are globally available over the Internet, providing almost any interested adversary a basic computer network exploitation or attack capability. Access to advanced weapons systems and innovative delivery systems could fundamentally change warfighting and dramatically increase an adversary's ability to threaten the United States.

Technology diffusion and access to advanced weapons and delivery systems have significant implications for military capabilities. The United States must have the ability to deny adversaries such disruptive technologies and weapons. However, the Armed Forces cannot focus solely on these threats and assume there are not other challenges on the horizon. Ensuring current readiness while continuing to transform and maintaining unchallenged military superiority will require investment. These are not mutually exclusive goals. The Armed Forces must remain ready to fight even as they transform and transform even as they fight. Adopting an "in-stride" approach to transformation – through rapid prototyping, field experimentation, organizational redesign and concept development – will ensure US military superiority remains unmatched. Such an approach requires effective balancing of resources to recapitalize critical capabilities and modernize some elements of the force to maintain readiness while investing in programs that extend US military advantages into the future.

D. Strategic Principles

Commanders must develop plans that ensure they retain the agility to contend with uncertainty, apply effects decisively and integrate actions with other government agencies and multinational partners. Combatant commanders should consider these principles when planning and conducting operations. These principles guide the development of joint operations concepts and the capabilities the joint force requires.

1. *Agility*

It is imperative that the Armed Forces retain the ability to contend with the principal characteristic of the security environment – uncertainty. Agility is the ability to rapidly deploy, employ, sustain and redeploy capabilities in geographically separated and environmentally diverse regions. As commanders conduct operations they must consider the effects of surprise and the possibility that their forces may have to transition from one type or phase of an operation to another quickly, or conduct phases simultaneously, regardless of location. Agility, as a planning principle, allows commanders to conduct simultaneous missions while retaining the ability to respond to emerging crises. Agility is key to quickly seizing the initiative across the range of military operations and ensuring the Armed Forces can act swiftly and decisively to protect US interests.

2. Decisiveness

Decisiveness allows combatant commanders to overwhelm adversaries, control situations and achieve definitive outcomes. Decisiveness requires tailored packages of joint capabilities designed to achieve specific effects and accomplish objectives. Achieving decisiveness may not require large force deployments but rather employing capabilities in innovative ways. Transforming the Armed Forces' capacity to mass effects while retaining the ability to mass forces, if needed, is key to achieving decisiveness. By focusing on decisive outcomes, combatant commanders can more precisely define the effects they must generate and determine the capabilities they require.

3. Integration

Commanders must ensure military activities are integrated effectively with the application of other instruments of national and international power to provide focus and unity of effort. Integration focuses on fusing and synchronizing military operations among the Services, other government agencies, the commercial sector, non-governmental organizations and those of partners abroad. Integration does not preclude the unilateral use of force, but rather seeks to ensure unity of effort and maximize the contribution of partners. Enabling multinational partners through security cooperation and other engagement activities enhances the ability of the Armed Forces to not only prevent conflict and deter aggression but also supports combatant commanders' plans to quickly undertake operations over great distances and in sometimes overlapping conflicts.

Agility, decisiveness, and integration support simultaneous operations, the application of overmatching power[3] and the fusion of US military power with other instruments of power. These principles stress speed, allowing US commanders to exploit an enemy's vulnerabilities, rapidly seize the initiative and achieve endstates. They support the concept of surging capabilities from widely dispersed locations to mass effects against an adversary's centers of gravity to achieve objectives. Our strategic principles guide the application of military power to protect, prevent and prevail in ways that contribute to longer-term national goals and objectives.

II. National Military Objectives

The 2004 NDS establishes four strategic objectives: secure the United States from direct attack; secure strategic access and maintain global freedom of action; establish security conditions conducive to a favorable international order; and strengthen alliances and partnerships to contend with common challenges. The NMS establishes

---

[3] Overmatching power is the precise application of combat power to foreclose enemy options and rapidly seize the initiative to achieve conclusive victories.

three supporting military objectives: to **protect the United States** against external attacks and aggression; **prevent conflict and surprise attack**; and **prevail against adversaries**. These are the ends of the strategy and help to assure allies and friends, dissuade adversaries and deter aggression and coercion while ensuring the Armed Forces remain ready to defeat adversaries should deterrence and dissuasion fail. They serve as benchmarks to assess levels of risk and help to define the types and amounts of military capabilities required.

Joint operating concepts (JOCs), currently under development, support each objective and link specific tasks to programmatic actions as well as guide the development of plans and the execution of operations. The current set of JOCs – **Homeland Security**, **Stability Operations**, **Strategic Deterrence** and **Major Combat Operations** – represent related actions that support all of the NMS objectives. While some of the JOCs may focus on specific elements of the strategy, success requires integrated action and unity of effort across each of the concepts. Although military objectives have enduring elements, the ways to achieve those goals must evolve through experimentation, operational experience, and the development of transformational capabilities.

Several considerations will guide combatant commanders in their planning. First, NMS objectives are interrelated and require the application of capabilities across the tactical, operational and strategic spectrum. Each of the objectives will generally involve collaborative efforts with other agencies and departments in the US government. Second, commanders will need to develop plans to achieve objectives simultaneously. The ability to conduct simultaneous operations ensures the United States retains its initiative even during multiple operations. Finally, commanders cannot rely solely on reactive measures and a robust defensive posture to accomplish objectives. This strategy requires a posture of anticipatory self-defense, which reflects the need for prepared and proportional responses to imminent aggression. When directed, commanders will preempt in self-defense those adversaries that pose an unmistakable threat of grave harm and which are not otherwise deterrable.

A. Protect the United States

Today, our first priority is to protect the United States. Joint forces help to secure the United States from direct attack through military activities overseas, planning and execution of homeland defense and support to civil authorities. Our experience in the WOT reinforces the fact that protecting the Nation and its global interests

---

Applying Strategic Principles

Strategic agility, integration and decisiveness allow the Armed Forces to move at great speed and distance to undertake combat operations quickly in sometimes overlapping conflicts. They guide the development of tailored, joint operations concepts that define how the Armed Forces employ capabilities across the range of military operations.

---

requires more than passive defensive measures. The threats posed by terrorist groups and rogue states, especially those that gain access to WMD/E, mandate an active defense-in-depth. Achieving this objective requires actions to counter threats overseas and close to their source; to secure our air, sea, space and land territorial approaches; and at home to defend against direct attacks. When directed, the Armed Forces provide military support to civil authorities, including capabilities to manage the consequences of an attack.

Countering Threats Close to their Source. Our primary line of defense remains well forward. Forces operating in key regions are essential to the defense of the United States and to the protection of allies and US interests. Our theater security activities with multinational partners provide access to information and intelligence critical to anticipating and understanding new threats. This access supports the ability of the United States to project power against threats and support the establishment of an environment that reduces the conditions that foster extremist ideologies. Our forces, including those rotationally deployed and those stationed forward, will work cooperatively with other nations to encourage regional partners to eliminate threats and patrol ungoverned space. More directly, deployed military units will work closely with international partners and other US government agencies to take the battle to the enemy – engaging terrorist forces, terrorist collaborators and those governments harboring terrorists.

Protecting Strategic Approaches. The JOC for "Homeland Security" includes tasks to protect the United States from direct attack while securing the air, sea, land and space approaches to the United States. We will join the efforts of multinational partners and other US government agencies to form an integrated defense of the air, land, sea and space approaches in and around US sovereign territory. Protecting these strategic approaches requires persistent surveillance that allows the United States to identify, continuously track and interdict potential threats. This integrated defense is essential to securing strategic access and retaining US freedom of action.

Defensive Actions at Home. While we will attempt to counter threats close to their source and interdict them along the strategic approaches, we must retain the ability to defend the United States from an attack that penetrates our forward defenses. At home the Armed Forces must defend the United States against air and missile attacks, terrorism and other direct attacks. As necessary, the Armed Forces will protect critical infrastructure that supports our ability to project military power. When directed, the Armed Forces will temporarily employ military capabilities to support law enforcement agencies during special events. During emergencies the Armed Forces may provide military support to civil authorities in mitigating the consequences of an attack or other catastrophic event when civilian responders are overwhelmed. Military responses under these conditions require a streamlined chain-of-command that integrates the unique capabilities of active and reserve military components and civilian responders. Effective defense in the face of adaptive adversaries will also require the exploitation of future technologies to improve capabilities to rapidly detect, assess and interdict WMD/E and emerging threats.

Creating a Global Anti-Terrorism Environment. In addition to defending the US homeland and supporting civil authorities, our strategy will diminish the conditions that permit terrorism to flourish. To defeat terrorists we will support national and partner nation efforts to deny state sponsorship, support, and sanctuary to terrorist organizations. We will work to deny terrorists safe haven in failed states and ungoverned regions. Working with other nations' militaries and other governmental agencies, the Armed Forces help to establish favorable security conditions and increase the capabilities of partners. The relationships developed in these interactions contribute to a global antiterrorism environment that further reduces threats to the

United States, its allies and its interests. For example, intelligence partnerships with other nations can take advantage of foreign expertise and areas of focus and provide access to previously denied areas. These relationships are essential mission components to protecting the United States, contributing to deterrence and conflict prevention, as well as preventing surprise attacks.

B. Prevent Conflict and Surprise Attacks

The United States must prevent conflict and surprise attacks through actions that deter aggression and coercion while retaining the capability to act promptly in defending the nation. Preventing conflict and deterring aggression rely in large part on an integrated overseas presence. Overseas, US forces permanently based in strategically important areas, rotationally deployed forward in support of regional objectives, and temporarily deployed during contingencies convey a credible message that the United States remains committed to preventing conflict. These forces also clearly demonstrate that the United States will react forcefully should an adversary threaten the United States, its interests, allies and partners. The United States must remain vigilant in identifying conditions that can lead to conflict in anticipating adversary actions and in reacting more swiftly than in the past. The Joint Force will deploy forward with a purpose – on the ground, in the air, in space and at sea – and work with other nations to promote security and to deter aggression. Preventing conflict and surprise attacks requires that the Armed Forces take action to ensure strategic access, establish favorable security conditions and work to increase the capabilities of partners to protect common security interests.

Forward Posture and Presence. Increasing the capabilities of partners and their willingness to cooperate in operations that ensure regional security requires an integrated, global view of our long-term strategy and enhancements to our overseas military posture. Combatant commanders, employing a mix of forward stationed, rotational and temporarily deployed capabilities tailored to perform specific missions, improve our ability to act within and across borders, strengthen the role of partners and expand joint and multinational capabilities. Posture and presence enhancements also serve to assure our friends; improve the ability to prosecute the WOT; deter, dissuade and defeat other threats; and support transformation. These changes, developed in anticipation of future threats, help to ensure strategic access to key regions and lines of communications critical to US security and sustaining operations throughout the battlespace. Within the process of adjusting our overseas presence, combatant commanders must develop and recommend posture adjustments that enable expeditionary, joint, and multinational forces to act promptly and globally while establishing favorable security conditions. The value and utility of having forces forward goes beyond winning on the battlefield. Employing forces in instances short of war demonstrates the United States' willingness to lead and encourages others to help defend, preserve and extend the peace.

Promote Security. The visible and purposeful presence of US military capabilities is an integral part of an active global strategy to ensure security and stability. Military forces engage in security cooperation (SC) activities to establish important military interactions, building trust and confidence between the United States and its multinational partners. These relatively small investments often produce results that far exceed their cost. SC complements other national-level efforts to prevent conflict and promote mutual security interests. These activities encourage nations to develop, modernize and transform their own capabilities, thereby increasing the capabilities of partners and helping them to help themselves. SC helps resolve doctrinal employment differences among military counterparts, enhances important intelligence and communication linkages and facilitates rapid crisis response. Active SC contributes to stability in key areas of the world while dissuading potential adversaries from adopting courses of action that threaten stability and security. In this way, we facilitate the integration of military operations with allies, contribute to regional stability, reduce underlying conditions that foment extremism and set the conditions for future success.

Deterring Aggression. Deterrence rests on an adversary understanding that the United States has an unquestioned ability to deny strategic objectives and to impose severe consequences in response to hostile or potentially hostile actions. Deterring aggression and coercion must be anticipatory in nature to prevent the catastrophic impact of attacks using biological, chemical or nuclear weapons on civilian population centers in the United States or in partner nations. The Armed Forces have the capability to exercise flexible deterrent options (FDOs) with appropriate combat power to defuse a crisis or force an adversary to reevaluate its courses of action. Combatant commanders build upon the capabilities of early arriving FDOs to support the swift defeat of an adversary when necessary. Moreover, they employ capabilities to establish favorable security conditions in which other, non-military FDOs can succeed. Effective deterrence requires a strategic communication plan that emphasizes the willingness of the United States to employ force in defense of its interests. The participation of combatant commanders is essential in developing a strategic communication plan that conveys US intent and objectives, and ensures the success of the plan by countering adversary disinformation and misinformation. Such strategic communication can help avoid conflict or deescalate tensions among adversaries.

The United States requires a broad set of options to discourage aggression and coercion. Nuclear capabilities continue to play an important role in deterrence by providing military options to deter a range of threats, including the use of WMD/E and large-scale conventional forces. Additionally, the extension of a credible nuclear deterrent to allies has been an important nonproliferation tool that has removed incentives for allies to develop and deploy nuclear forces. Deterring aggression by a wider range of adversaries requires transforming existing US strategic nuclear forces into a new triad composed of a diverse portfolio of capabilities. This new model for strategic deterrence includes non-nuclear and nuclear strike forces, active and passive defenses, as well as infrastructure to build and maintain the force. Improvements and enhancements to non-nuclear strike capabilities, information operations, command and control, intelligence and space forces will contribute to a more robust and effective deterrent capability. Future advances in targeting and precision will provide the capabilities necessary to defeat a wider range of targets while reducing collateral damage.

Preventing Surprise Attacks. Military forces can no longer focus solely on responding to aggression. The potentially horrific consequences of an attack against the United States demand action to secure the Nation from direct attack by eliminating certain threats before they can strike. Deterring threats and preventing surprise attacks will place increasing demands on intelligence assets, the agility and decisiveness of the force and the ability to work time-critical issues in the interagency setting. Preventative missions require shared, "actionable" intelligence, and rules of engagement that allow commanders to make timely decisions. This decision making process stresses collaboration, speed and responsiveness – key ingredients required when exploiting time-sensitive opportunities as they arise, especially against mobile, time critical targets. These missions require exacting analysis and synthesis of intelligence gathered by a combination of capabilities, including human and technical collectors. These operations will generally involve coordinated efforts with other agencies and departments in the US government, placing a premium on information sharing, intelligence fusion and collaborative planning.

JOCs for **stability operations** and **strategic deterrence** are essential to how combatant commanders employ forces before, during and after conflict. Preventing conflict requires the capability to perform stability operations to maintain or re-establish order, promote peace and security or improve existing conditions. This will involve close coordination with other elements of the US government and multinational partners. Such actions reduce the underlying conditions that foster terrorism and the extremist ideologies that support terrorism. Stability operations create favorable security conditions that allow other instruments of national and international power to succeed. Preventing conflict and surprise attacks is a key element to protecting the United States from direct attack and helps to set the conditions in which the Armed Forces can prevail against adversaries.

C. Prevail Against Adversaries

When necessary, the Armed Forces will defeat adversaries. Developments in the security environment necessitate a Joint Force that can achieve tactical and operational success and prevail in a manner that establishes favorable security conditions and ensures enduring victories. Terrorist attacks demonstrate that conflict is not limited to geographic borders and that defeating root causes of terrorism requires a total national effort. The United States will constantly strive to enlist the support of the international community and increase the capabilities of partners to contend with common challenges, but will not hesitate to act alone, if necessary.

Swiftly Defeat Adversaries. Some operation plans will focus on achieving a limited set of objectives. Commanders' plans to swiftly defeat adversaries will include options to: alter the unacceptable behavior or policies of states; rapidly seize the initiative or prevent conflict escalation; deny an adversary sanctuary, defeat his offensive capabilities or objectives; and provide support to post-conflict stability. In each case, the Joint Force must combine speed, agility and superior warfighting ability to generate decisive effects. Moving forces into multiple geographic locations will require assured strategic access as well as strategic and tactical lift systems robust enough to conduct and sustain multiple, simultaneous operations. Swiftly defeating adversaries in overlapping operations will require the ability to quickly reconstitute, reconfigure and redeploy forces to conduct another campaign.

Win Decisively. Where necessary, commanders' plans will include options to rapidly transition to a campaign to win decisively and achieve enduring results. The capabilities required for major combat operations must be applicable to the full spectrum of threats ranging from state to non-state adversaries employing traditional and/or asymmetric capabilities. A campaign to win decisively will include actions to: destroy an adversary's military capabilities through the integrated application of air, ground, maritime, space and information capabilities; and potentially remove adversary regimes when directed. Such campaigns require capabilities for conventional warfighting, unconventional warfare, homeland security, stability and post-conflict operations, countering terrorism and security cooperation activities.

Stability Operations. Winning decisively will require synchronizing and integrating major combat operations, stability operations and significant post-conflict interagency operations to establish conditions of stability and security favorable to the United States. The Joint Force must be able to transition from major combat operations to stability operations and to conduct those operations simultaneously. At the operational level, military post-conflict operations will integrate conflict termination objectives with diplomatic, economic, financial, intelligence, law enforcement and information efforts. Joint forces will, where appropriate, synchronize and coordinate their operations and activities with international partners and non-governmental organizations. These missions render other instruments of national power more effective and set the conditions for long-term regional stability and sustainable development.

The JOCs for **major combat operations** and **stability operations** are complementary and must be fully integrated and synchronized in campaign planning. These concepts allow the Joint Force to conduct sequential, parallel or simultaneous operations throughout the physical and information domains of the global battlespace. The goal of these JOCs is to sustain increased operating tempo, place continuous pressure on the adversary and synchronize military action with the application of other instruments of national power.

III. A Joint Force for Mission Success

The objectives of protect, prevent and prevail provide the foundation for defining military capabilities and creating a joint force that can contend effectively with uncertainty. They support a capabilities-based approach that focuses on how adversaries will fight in the future rather than on which specific adversaries we may fight. The Armed Forces must have the ability to defeat opponents that possess WMD/E, combine both low-tech and high-tech capabilities and merge traditional and asymmetric capabilities in an attempt to overcome US military advantages.

Defeating adaptive adversaries requires flexible, modular and deployable joint forces with the ability to combine the strengths of individual Services, combatant commands, other government agencies and multinational partners. Joint forces will require new levels of interoperability and systems that are "born joint," i.e., conceptualized and designed with joint architectures and acquisition strategies. This level of interoperability ensures that technical, doctrinal and cultural barriers do not limit the ability of joint commanders to achieve objectives. The goal is to design joint force capabilities that increase the range of options – from kinetic to non-kinetic – available to the President and Secretary of Defense.

A. Desired Attributes

The challenge over the next decade will be to develop and enhance joint capabilities in a time of global war, finite resources and multiple commitments. While the United States enjoys an overwhelming qualitative advantage today, sustaining and increasing this advantage will require transformation - a transformation achieved by combining technology, intellect and cultural changes across the joint community. The Armed Forces must be able to evaluate challenges, leverage innovation and technology and act decisively in pursuit of national goals.

Joint forces operating in this complex battlespace must be fully integrated and adaptable to anticipate and counter the most dangerous threats. They will also require expeditionary capabilities with highly mobile forces skilled in flexible, adaptive planning and decentralized execution even when operating from widely dispersed locations. Operational planning and execution requires decision superiority and the prerequisite authority to take actions and exploit fleeting opportunities. The joint force will use superior intelligence and the power of information technologies to increase decision superiority, precision and lethality of the force. A networked force capable of decision superiority can collect, analyze and rapidly disseminate intelligence and other relevant information from the national to tactical levels, then use that information to decide and act faster than opponents.

> **Joint Force Attributes**
> **(Characteristics Describing the Joint Force)**
>
> - **Fully Integrated**—functions and capabilities focused toward a unified purpose.
> - **Expeditionary**—rapidly deployable, employable and sustainable throughout the global battlespace.
> - **Networked**—linked and synchronized in time and purpose.
> - **Decentralized**—integrated capabilities operating in a joint manner at lower echelons.
> - **Adaptable**—prepared to quickly respond with the appropriate capabilities mix.
> - **Decision superiority**—better-informed decisions implemented faster than an adversary can react.
> - **Lethality**—destroy an adversary and/or his systems in all conditions.
>
> *Joint Operations Concepts*

A joint force with these attributes requires more than technological solutions. It relies on disciplined, skilled, dedicated and professional service men and women. It also requires informed and empowered joint leaders who combine superior technical skills, operational experience, intellectual understanding and cultural expertise to employ capabilities and perform critical joint functions. A joint force, possessing the attributes described and comprised of highly motivated professionals, will produce creative solutions to the most difficult problems.

B. Functions and Capabilities

Inherent in each military objective is a series of functions that the Joint Force must perform. Commanders derive their tasks and define required capabilities through an analysis of these functions and the concepts that describe how the Armed Forces will perform them. Capabilities that allow the Joint Force to perform these functions result from combinations of joint doctrine, organization, training programs, materiel solutions, leadership, personnel and facilities.

1. Applying Force

The application of military force to achieve the objectives of the NMS is the primary task of the Armed Forces. It requires the integrated use of maneuver and engagement to create precisely defined effects. Force application includes force movement to gain positional and temporal advantage to rapidly seize the initiative and complicate an adversary's defensive plans. Force application integrates air, land, sea, special operations, information and space capabilities. It also requires unprecedented levels of persistence that allow commanders, even in a high-threat environment, to assess results against mission objectives, adjust capabilities accordingly and reengage as required.

Applying force requires power projection assets to move capabilities rapidly, employ them precisely and sustain them even when adversaries employ anti-access and counter power projection strategies. Such power projection requires assured access to theaters of operation and enhanced expeditionary capabilities that support operational maneuver from strategic distances. Strong regional alliances and coalitions enhance expeditionary capabilities by providing physical access to host nation infrastructure and other support. They also provide access to regional intelligence that enables the precise application of military capabilities and allows the United States to focus combat power more effectively at the critical time and place. Achieving shared situational awareness with allies and partners will require compatible information systems and security processes that protect sensitive information without degrading the ability of multinational partners to operate effectively with US elements. Such information and intelligence sharing helps builds trust and confidence essential to strong international partnerships.

Force application focuses more on generating the right effects to achieve objectives than on generating overwhelming numbers of forces. The application of force against widely dispersed adversaries, including transnational terrorist organizations, will require improved intelligence collection and analysis systems. Effective global strike to damage, neutralize or destroy any objective results from a combination of precision and maneuver and the integration of new technologies, doctrine and organizations. Defeating the most dangerous threats will require persistence in force application that allows strikes against time-sensitive and time-critical targets. Ensuring capabilities are positioned and ready to conduct strikes against these targets requires the ability to sustain operations over time and across significant distances.

2. Deploying and Sustaining Military Capabilities

Force application in multiple overlapping operations will challenge sustainment capabilities. Sustaining such operations requires the ability to support forces operating in and from austere or unimproved forward locations. Additionally, the increasing importance of mobility will necessitate more expeditionary logistics capabilities. Focused logistics provides the right personnel, equipment and supplies in the right quantities and at the right place and time. Such focused logistics capabilities will place a premium on networking to create a seamless end-to-end logistics system that synchronizes all aspects of the deployment and distribution processes.

Overlapping major combat operations place major demands on strategic mobility. Achieving objectives in such operations requires robust sealift, airlift, aerial refueling and pre-positioned assets. Strategic mobility that supports these operations also requires supporting equipment to store, move and distribute materiel and an information infrastructure to provide real-time visibility of the entire logistics chain.

Sustainment includes force generation and management activities that ensure the long-term viability of the force. Force generation includes recruiting, training, educating and retaining highly qualified people in the Active and Reserve Components as well as within the DOD civilian and contracted workforce. These personnel must have the right skill sets to apply joint doctrine within their organizations. Force generation requirements must include planning, programming, acquisition, maintenance, repair and recapitalization of equipment and infrastructure to maintain readiness.

Force management contributes to improving readiness levels even during high-intensity operations. It considers the effects of modernization and transformation on unit availability, readiness and integration. Force management policies, including force rotation policies that reduce stress on the joint force, evolve from continuous assessments of operational requirements. They also help to determine the appropriate locations, capabilities and associated infrastructure required to support multiple, simultaneous operations. Force management policies help define the right mix of Active and Reserve Component forces and ensure a proper balance of capabilities.

3. Securing Battlespace

The Armed Forces must have the ability to operate across the air, land, sea, space and cyberspace domains of the battlespace. Armed Forces must employ military capabilities to ensure access to these domains to protect the Nation, forces in the field and US global interests. The non-linear nature of the current security environment requires multi-layered active and passive measures to counter numerous diverse conventional and asymmetric threats. These include conventional weapons, ballistic and cruise missiles and WMD/E. They also include threats in cyberspace aimed at networks and data critical to US information-enabled systems. Such threats require a comprehensive concept of deterrence encompassing traditional adversaries, terrorist networks and rogue states able to employ any range of capabilities.

The Armed Forces require new capabilities to detect and interdict a wide range of threats close to their source and throughout the strategic approaches. The availability of intelligence and dual use technology to a wider variety of potential adversaries poses an increasing danger, providing them the ability to interrupt or exploit US information systems. Adversaries may find new and innovative ways to combine capabilities into effective weapons and enhance their ability to threaten the United States. Military forces must have both the means and established rules of engagement to take action

16

ranging from active counter proliferation to military action that supports non-proliferation policies. Securing battlespace will require cooperative activities with other government agencies and multinational partners to deny the use of these capabilities and to counter asymmetric attacks. This requires doctrine, tools and training to more effectively synchronize military capabilities with non-DOD assets.

Consequence management capabilities are essential in the aftermath of an attack, especially an attack with WMD/E. Such capabilities limit damage and casualties and include actions to counter the effects of WMD/E or the intentional or unintentional release of toxic chemicals following military operations. Consequence management helps restore affected areas through actions that contain, neutralize and decontaminate weapon agents. When directed, the Joint Force will extend consequence management assistance to allies and other security partners.

Military operations require information assurance that guarantees access to information systems and their products and the ability to deny adversaries access to the same. Securing the battlespace includes actions to safeguard information and command and control systems that support the precise application of force and sustainment activities that ensure persistence across the full range of military operations. Securing battlespace ensures the ability of the Armed Forces to collect, process, analyze and disseminate all-source intelligence and other relevant information that contribute to decision superiority.

4. Achieving Decision Superiority

Decision superiority – the process of making decisions better and faster than an adversary – is essential to executing a strategy based on speed and flexibility. Decision superiority requires new ways of thinking about acquiring, integrating, using and sharing information. It necessitates new ideas for developing architectures for command, control, communications and computers (C4) as well as the intelligence, surveillance and reconnaissance assets that provide knowledge of adversaries. Decision superiority requires precise information of enemy and friendly dispositions, capabilities, and activities, as well as other data relevant to successful campaigns. Battlespace awareness, combined with responsive command and control systems, supports dynamic decision-making and turns information superiority into a competitive advantage adversaries cannot match.

Persistent surveillance, ISR management, collaborative analysis and on-demand dissemination facilitate battlespace awareness. Developing the intelligence products to support this level of awareness requires collection systems and assured access to air, land, sea and space-based sensors. Human collectors are a critical element in the collection system; they provide the ability to discern the intention of adversaries and produce actionable intelligence for plans and orders. Intelligence analysts operating well forward must have the ability to reach back to comprehensive, integrated databases and to horizontally integrate information and intelligence. The entire system must be supported by effective counterintelligence capabilities that deny an adversary access to critical information.

Battlespace awareness requires the ability to share relevant information with other government agencies and allies. Such information sharing requires multi-level security capabilities that allow multinational partners and other government agencies to access and use relevant information while reducing the probability of compromise. Seamless multi-level security access will empower distributed command and control and provide increased transparency in multinational operations. Decisions to apply force in multiple, widely dispersed locations require highly flexible and adaptive joint command and control processes. Commanders must communicate decisions to subordinates, rapidly develop alternative courses of action, generate required effects, assess results and conduct appropriate follow-on operations.

The Joint Force requires the ability to conduct information operations, including electronic warfare, computer network operations, military deception, psychological operations and operations security that enable information superiority. Information operations must be adaptive – tailorable to specific audiences and requirements and flexible enough to accommodate operational adjustments. Should deterrence fail, information operations can disrupt an enemy's network and communications-dependent weapons, infrastructure and command and control and battlespace management functions. Information operations, both offensive and defensive, are key to ensuring US freedom of action across the battlespace.

A decision superior joint force must employ decision-making processes that allow commanders to attack time-sensitive and time-critical targets. Dynamic decision-making brings together organizations, planning processes, technical systems and commensurate authorities that support informed decisions. Such decisions require networked command and control capabilities and a tailored common operating picture of the battlespace. Networking must also provide increased transparency in multinational operations and support the integration of other government agencies and multinational partners into joint operations. Force application, sustainment and actions to secure battlespace will rely on these capabilities.

IV. Force Design and Size

A. Force Design and Size

The 2004 NDS directs a force sized to defend the homeland, deter forward in and from four regions, and conduct two, overlapping "swift defeat" campaigns. Even when committed to a limited number of lesser contingencies, the force must be able to "win decisively" in one of the two campaigns. This "1-4-2-1" force-sizing construct places a premium on increasingly innovative and efficient methods to achieve objectives. The construct establishes mission parameters for the most demanding set of potential scenarios and encompasses the full range of military operations. It does not represent a specific set of scenarios nor reflect temporary conditions. As a result, planners and programmers should take into account the following implications of the construct.

Baseline Security Posture. Combatant commanders will perform their missions within a baseline security posture that includes the WOT, ongoing operations and other day-to-day activities to which US forces remain committed and from which they are unlikely to disengage entirely. The extremely demanding circumstances associated with the ongoing WOT are likely to endure for the foreseeable future. Because post-conflict and WOT operations are likely of long duration and will vary in intensity, planners must account for the capabilities required to achieve campaign objectives. Commanders must develop options to achieve success given this baseline security posture and identify capability trade-offs necessary to manage increased risks.

Adequacy and Presence. Determining the size of the force requires assessing the adequacy of the force to meet current and future challenges and the optimization of current end strength and force/capabilities mix. Sizing the force must consider the allocation, location, distribution and support of overseas forces. Sizing must account for sustaining permanently stationed, rotationally and temporarily deployed forward forces; overseas infrastructure; and resources, including the strategic lift and security necessary to project and sustain these capabilities over time. Some crises may prove more difficult than anticipated or may escalate quickly. Reducing this risk and ensuring the ability of the Armed Forces to prevail will require "early-entry" capabilities forward for rapid action, while relying on surge capacity to provide follow-on forces.

Disengagement. While the force-planning construct assumes that the United States will disengage from some contingencies when faced with a second overlapping campaign, there may be some lesser contingencies that the United States is unwilling or unable to terminate quickly. There may be forces conducting long-term stability operations to reestablish favorable post conflict security conditions from which the United States cannot disengage. Under such circumstance some important capabilities may not be readily available at the outset of a subsequent conflict. Combatant commanders must consider this possibility when preparing to undertake operations, as many of the same capabilities critical to campaigns are required to conduct lesser contingency operations.

Escalation. Actions to size the force must take into account the fact that lesser contingencies have the potential to escalate to more demanding campaigns. Providing a wider range of military options during crises requires a force sized for a probable level of commitment across the full range of military operations – while ensuring that continued commitment to such contingencies does not preclude the ability of the United States to conduct major campaigns.

Force Generation and Transformation. Force sizing and design must look beyond current operations. The health of the force rests on the ability to generate, sustain and transform capabilities over the long term. Sizing the force must include an appreciation of the force requirements to support ongoing training activities, "in-stride" transformation and other programs that may restrict the availability of forces and capabilities provided to combatant commanders. Assessments of acceptable levels of risk will dictate the type and kinds of capabilities that Armed Forces must possess to surge to meet the most demanding set of requirements.

B. Risk and Force Assessments

Given current force levels and appropriate resources, this strategy is executable. While US conventional military capabilities are, and will likely remain, unmatched for the foreseeable future, demands on the Armed Forces across the range of military operations remain considerable. Pursuing the WOT, conducting stability operations in Afghanistan and Iraq, ensuring power projection from the Homeland and sustaining global commitments while protecting the long-term health of the Armed Forces will require actions to mitigate risk. Commanders must develop options to balance demands like transformation, modernization and recapitalization that, if unrealized over the longer-term, could make it increasingly difficult to execute this military strategy. Annex A provides a complete assessment of risk and mitigation options.

At present, the Armed Forces remain optimized for high-intensity conflict and combat operations in mature theaters. Our experience in the WOT has provided insights on both the strengths and deficiencies in our concepts for employing military force as well as some of the capabilities the Armed Forces must improve. The Armed Forces remain fully capable of conducting major combat operations and a range of lesser contingencies. While we have adapted these forces successfully in OEF and OIF, success in future operations will require further and more substantive changes. Additionally, changes in the security environment will necessitate adaptations in the Joint Force. These changes include evolution of threats and an assessment of the ability of our allies and partners to contribute capabilities in support of US operational requirements. Annex B contains a more detailed regional assessment and includes projected allied and partner contributions to achieving the objectives of the NMS.

V. Joint Vision for Future Warfighting

The attributes and capabilities of the Joint Force provide the foundation for the force of the future. They provide the basis for adjustments to organizational design and doctrine as changes and challenges arise. They support the goals of the Department of Defense in ways that complement other instruments of national power. The goal is full spectrum dominance (FSD) – the ability to control any situation or defeat any adversary across the range of military operations.

A. Full Spectrum Dominance

FSD is the overarching concept for applying force today and provides a vision for future joint operations. Achieving FSD requires the Armed Forces to focus transformation efforts on key capability areas that enhance the ability of the joint force to achieve success across the range of military operations. FSD requires joint military capabilities, operating concepts, functional concepts and critical enablers adaptable to diverse conditions and objectives.

FSD recognizes the need to integrate military activities with those of other government agencies, the importance of interoperability with allies and other partners

Focusing Transformation

The 2004 National Defense Strategy identifies eight capability areas that "provide a transformation focus for the Department."

- Strengthening Intelligence
- Protecting Critical Bases of Operation
- Operating from the Commons: Space, International Waters and Airspace, and Cyberspace
- Projecting and Sustaining US Forces in Distant Anti-Access Environments
- Denying Enemies Sanctuary
- Conducting Network-Centric Operations
- Improving Proficiency for Irregular Warfare
- Increasing Capabilities of Partners – International and Domestic

and the criticality of transforming in-stride. FSD will serve to strengthen the trust and confidence that exists among Service components by acknowledging their interdependence and developing concepts that reduce gaps and seams among organizations. It requires a capabilities-based approach that balances near-term capabilities with longer-term requirements and incorporates a global perspective on military and strategic risk. This integrative concept ensures military forces possess capabilities to rapidly conduct globally dispersed, simultaneous operations; foreclose adversary options; and, if required, generate the desired effects necessary to decisively defeat adversaries.

Along with technological solutions to improve joint warfighting, we must also examine our doctrine, organizations, training systems, materiel procurement, leadership preparation, personnel programs and facilities to ensure military superiority. This requires a more holistic approach to countering today's threats and preparing for those likely to emerge in the future. Reducing lead times associated with research, development and fielding of new capabilities must be a priority. Such actions are essential to an in-stride approach to transforming the Joint Force and executing concepts for future joint warfighting. Research and development programs are equally important to FSD, providing a hedge against the more uncertain aspects of the security environment.

B. Initiatives

The Services and combatant commands are actively involved in a number of initiatives to ensure military superiority. US Armed Forces must remain superior to any other nation's while engaging in interagency and international efforts that continue to set the conditions to protect the United States and win the WOT. The following initiatives represent some of the ongoing activities that enhance joint warfighting and support transformation.

Organizational Adaptation. Adaptive organizations must be more modular and support rapid reconfiguration of joint capabilities for specific missions. Modular forces build on the core competencies of each Service component while enhancing the strength of joint operations. Organizational adaptation will require actions to balance Active and Reserve Components to sustain an appropriate mix of capabilities. Additionally, the creation of Standing Joint Force Headquarters (SJFHQ) will provide the core capability for a Joint Task Force (JTF) Headquarters within each combatant command. SJFHQs facilitate rapid employment of cross-service capabilities to respond to contingencies and crises around the world. Selectively manned, trained, and equipped, these SJFHQs will have the tools to operate effectively in any contingency. At the same time, the creation of a Joint National Training Capability will allow the Joint Force to train and gain experience at the tactical and operational levels of warfare. Once established, it will provide realistic training for joint forces and support battlespace awareness functions. This new training capability will better prepare the Joint Force for asymmetric challenges and a diverse array of threats.

Interagency Integration and Information Sharing. Implementing Counter-Terrorist (CT) Joint Interagency Coordination Groups (JIACGs) at five regional and two global combatant commands facilitates interagency integration. The JIACGs are multifunctional elements that have dramatically increased information sharing across the interagency community. Continuing the experimentation process supports the Armed Forces' goal to develop and field a "full spectrum" JIACG that will tap interagency expertise to address the many transnational issues facing the combatant commanders. In the near term the Armed Forces will facilitate information sharing and common situational awareness between elements of the JIACG with the DOD standard collaboration toolset that enables virtual collaboration. Interagency integration enables a strategic communications plan that includes elements of public affairs and public diplomacy. In addition to military information operations, this strategic communication plan ensures unity of themes and messages, emphasizes success, accurately confirms or refutes external reporting on US operations, and reinforces the legitimacy of US goals. Combatant commanders must be actively involved in the development, execution and support of this strategic communication campaign.

Global Information Grid. The DOD is further developing a fully interoperable, interagency-wide global information grid (GIG). The GIG has the potential to be the single most important enabler of information and decision superiority. The GIG supports the creation of a collaborative information environment that facilitates information sharing, effective synergistic planning, and execution of simultaneous, overlapping operations. It will be a globally interconnected, end-to-end set of information capabilities, associated processes, and personnel for collecting, processing, storing, disseminating and managing information on demand to defense policymakers, warfighters and support personnel. Other initiatives include the transformation of battlespace awareness systems to include the Operational Net Assessment (ONA) Concept, the Multinational Information Sharing (MNIS) Transformation Change Package (TCP) and several Advanced Concept Technology Demonstrations (ACTDs). They respectively address information and knowledge for decision-making; technical, policy, and organization issues; and innovative capabilities. These activities are among the ongoing efforts related to improving information sharing among coalition partners.

Enhancing Overseas Presence Posture. An integrated global presence and basing strategy provides the context for actions that enhance warfighting while strengthening and expanding the United State's network of partnerships. Such a strategy provides rationale for adjustments in permanent and rotational presence, prepositioned equipment, global sourcing and surge capabilities that support these goals. Posture adjustments must support winning the WOT while setting the conditions that will ensure an enduring peace. Enhancing US overseas presence and global footprint must improve the ability of regional forces to employ an expeditionary approach in response to regional and global contingencies. They must remain "scaleable," supporting plans to surge forces during crises when and where they are needed. Modifications to US overseas presence and posture must enhance the Armed Forces' ability to deal with uncertainty, enable rapid operations and allow forces to respond with greater speed than in the past. US overseas presence must also improve conditions in key regions and support conflict prevention. An integrated global presence and basing strategy serves to strengthen existing alliances while helping to create new partnerships. Strengthening regional alliances and coalitions helps to create favorable regional balances of power that help bring pressure to bear on hostile or uncooperative regimes. Multinational partnerships expand opportunities for coalition building through combined training, experimentation and transformation. An integrated global presence and basing strategy will expand the range of pre-conflict options to deter aggression and control conflict escalation while setting the conditions for a sustainable peace.

Joint Leader Development. We continue to improve joint professional military education to provide more joint experiences, education and training to warfighters – junior and senior officers and noncommissioned officers. At the senior officer level, a modified capstone course will increase the emphasis on jointness while preparing senior officers to lead joint task forces and other joint operations. For junior officers and noncommissioned officers, incorporating joint education and training early in their careers ensures future leaders will more effectively integrate tactical operations with interagency and multinational components.

VI. Conclusion

This strategy focuses the Armed Forces on winning the WOT and enhancing joint warfighting while supporting actions to create a joint, network-centric, distributed force, capable of full spectrum dominance. Achieving decision superiority and generating tailored effects across the battlespace allows the Joint Force to control any situation over a range of military operations. To succeed, the Armed Forces must integrate Service capabilities in new and innovative, reduce seams between combatant commands and develop more collaborative relationships with partners at home and abroad.

The NMS defines specific tasks for the Joint Force that allow commanders to assess military and strategic risk. It guides adjustments to plans and programs to generate, employ and sustain joint capabilities effectively. Additionally, it provides insights on operational matters, institutional issues, force management programs, future challenges and recommends courses of action to mitigate risk.

> **The Mission of the Armed Forces**
>
> In support of the objectives of the 2004 NDS the Armed Forces conduct military activities globally to:
>
> - **Protect** the United States against external attacks and aggression.
> - **Prevent** conflict and surprise attacks.
> - **Prevail** against adversaries.

While engaged in multiple worldwide operations to meet these requirements, the Armed Forces of the United States must maintain force quality, enhance joint warfighting capabilities and transform to meet the challenges of the 21st century. Executing this strategy will require a truly joint, full spectrum force – with a seamless mix of active forces, the Reserve Component, DOD civilians, and contracted workforce – fully grounded in a culture of innovation. It will require the highest quality people – disciplined, dedicated, professional – well trained, well educated, and well led.

Appropriately resourced, this strategy will achieve the goals of the NSS and 2004 NDS, effectively balancing military and strategic risk over the long term. It will enable us to counter the threats of today and transform the Joint Force to master the challenges of the future.